OXFORD:
THE UNIVERSITY
IN OLD PHOTOGRAPHS

KING ALFRED was only one of a series of personages, real or legendary, credited with founding the University. Only a hundred years ago was the myth (cultivated for centuries, especially at University College) finally demolished. This statue, taken down from the college and put in the Master's garden, was photographed in 1915, but has since vanished. (OL.)

OXFORD:
THE UNIVERSITY
IN OLD PHOTOGRAPHS

COLLECTED BY
JOHN RHODES

ALAN SUTTON
1988

Alan Sutton Publishing Limited
Brunswick Road · Gloucester

First published 1988

British Library Cataloguing in Publication Data

Rhodes, John, 1944–
Oxford: the university in old photographs.
1. Oxfordshire. Oxford. Universities:
University of Oxford, to 1973
I. Title
378.425'74'09

ISBN 0-86299-461-6

Front Cover Illustration:
Tourists in Tom Quad, Christ Church, c. 1905. (OM.)

Typesetting and origination by
Alan Sutton Publishing Limited.
Printed in Great Britain
by WBC Print Limited.

CONTENTS

INTRODUCTION

Oxford has always seemed worth illustrating, and we see it in the past through the eyes of its illustrators. Sixteenth-century Oxford is Bereblock's engravings; seventeenth-century Oxford is David Loggan's clean and meticulous records of college and university buildings, all crisp, regular and in good shape, invaluable as an historical record, but not how it must have really looked. Only with the series of aquatints for Ackermann's Oxford in the early nineteenth century (for grand buildings) and J.C. Buckler's careful records of lesser buildings, do we begin to get a real sense of Oxford as it was.

University people we must imagine from the portraits which look down from the walls of the Bodleian Library or of college halls, or from Rowlandson's cartoons of low university life. The view is through the eyes of the artist and engraver, composing the picture, over a number of days, to suit the sitter, the market and the current style. The market was composed of University people, especially the transitory student, the even more transitory tourist and all those interested in grand and ancient buildings, of which Oxford has a marvellous concentration.

The modern idea of the City and University is very similar; Oxford is old, spectacular and rather strange. A vast production of postcards, guide-books and other souvenirs all show this aspect of the University. The typical, ordinary or small-scale sides of life have not, until recently, been thought interesting or saleable.

Between these ends of the scale was a remarkable period when the new technique of photography reflected the city, in an immediate way, as it really was. Partly, there were the grand views of grand buildings in the traditional manner. For the first time though, we can see the buildings as people then saw them, in all their creeper-hung reality, decayed, softened and darkened by time. It is almost a shock to see familiar buildings, which we know in their crisply restored form, looking so apparently neglected, or at least looking their age. The Oxford of the 1970s and 80s has become all new again, as the massive programme of restoration makes the city look as it has never looked before, as if all built at the same time.

Initially, the streets look empty, very different from the well-populated and cheerful prints of the eighteenth and early nineteenth centuries. Early photographic techniques did not allow for the quick record of busy street scenes, and many of the views show Oxford as it might have looked in the vacations, if not actually taken then. The place must have been more active than it seems, with university and town people and a growing number, even then, of tourists.

People needed more careful posing. An extensive number of portrait photographs survive of university personalities (such as had before been recorded, as they continued to be, by the formal painted portrait), but now also of undergraduates, college servants and others, appearing for the first time as individuals or in informal groups. The formal group came too. Photography's ability was to capture a number of people in a single process, at one moment in time. From the 1860s until today the commercial photographer's bread and butter in Oxford has been the annual record of groups: the new undergraduates, the members of colleges, clubs and sports teams. Eventually activities could be captured, particularly those on the river; the astonishing crowds at Eight's Weeks, the packed spectators on college barges, punting and picnics. The record photograph became an automatic part of a whole range of activities in a way it no longer is. Posterity may have a clearer visual impression of the Victorian and Edwardian University than it has of today's.

The photographers themselves, shrouded under their black cloths, were a group which grew in Oxford to meet the demand. Photography was both new and easily accessible and there was plenty of work. An early pioneer was Edward Bracher, in the 1850s, with a shop at 26 High Street. By 1864 there were at least ten firms in Oxford, including Hills & Saunders, who long remained the most important photographers to the University from their premises in Cornmarket Street. One of their specialities was the production of albums recording the university careers of individuals, from school to Oxford, college groups, sports clubs, societies and dinners, which have been a valuable source of illustrations for this book.

Forty years later there were nearly twenty firms, among them Gillman & Co. of 107 St Aldates and James Soame of 101 High Street. Having come together, the firm continues as Gillman & Soame, University and School Group Photographers.

The most important photographer of the late nineteenth and early twentieth centuries was Henry William Taunt. He served his apprenticeship with Bracher, set up his own shop in 1868 and rapidly built up a successful business. In 1874 he took a shop in Broad Street where he stayed for twenty years. Taunt's particular love was the river, but in addition to river scenes he took a great range of subjects –

buildings, street scenes, ceremonies, gardens and groups. His are the most compelling of the photographs of the City and University in the late nineteenth and early twentieth centuries.

Of the amateurs, the best and best-known was Charles Lutwidge Dodgson, Mathematical Tutor of Christ Church, and one of the most important portrait photographers of the nineteenth century. The stories he told to Alice, daughter of Dean Liddell of Christ Church, ensured his fame as Lewis Carroll; his photographs of Alice and his other 'child-friends' are just part of a wonderful range of pictures of his fellow dons, students and the famous from the period after he took up photography in 1856. In the 1890s Oxford's first woman photographer, and another talented amateur, was Sarah Acland, daughter of Sir Henry, who began to take photographs as a hobby and made portraits of her father's friends and visitors at the Acland home at 40 Broad Street. A particular friend was Sir William Herschel, ex-Indian Civil Servant, President of the Oxford Camera Club and with a keen interest in developing colour photography.

What all these photographs sadly lack, of course, is colour. Black and white, they show the University in a century of great change. More happened in the University in the century between the 1840s and the 1940s than in any previous time. It was a period of new rigour in intellectual life, a new concern with standards, a new religious fervour, a concern for new subjects and disciplines. Oxford was setting out to take its place in the modern world. The old and comfortable eighteenth century was replaced bit by bit, intellectually and physically. Oxford became less clerical and aristocratic, gradually more liberal and concerned with real merit. The figures in this were many, but among them were Benjamin Jowett, Master of Balliol from 1870, Dean Liddell of Christ Church and his friend Henry Acland, champion of science and medicine. Examinations became written, rather than often ridiculously easy oral tests. College numbers expanded. Women's halls were set up, though their students were not able to take degrees until the 1920s. There was interest in education in a wider sense, with the setting up of systems of open University teaching to external students.

The effects of all this can be seen. Colleges grew in physical size, renewing old buildings or building new ones, usually at the expense of the old houses of the town. Brand new colleges were established, Keble being the first but followed by others, a process continuing through the twentieth century. The old schools of the seventeenth century outgrew their space and new Examination Schools were built in High Street to provide for University lectures. A new Ashmolean took on the housing of the University's art and archaeology collections. The University Museum of the 1850s became a centre for scientific study of the natural world, to which the Pitt Rivers Museum in the 1880s, for the study of mankind, became the first addition in the process which created the Science Area. The new Oxford attracted endowments. Lord Nuffield became one of its most generous benefactors, with Nuffield College and his medical foundations all now important parts of the University.

Year by year not all of this can have seemed very apparent; it happened slowly against the background of college and university life, study, entertainment and leisure, revealed in these photographs.

SECTION ONE

Setting and Approaches

THE CITY IS BEST SEEN from the nearby hills to the east and west. This view over the trees of Headington Hill Hall was taken by Henry Taunt, possibly in the 1890s. (OL.)

THE EASTERN ENTRANCE TO THE CITY, over Magdalen Bridge and beneath the great bell tower of Magdalen College. The photograph is c. 1880, just before the widening of the bridge to accommodate more traffic. (OL.)

THE GROWTH OF TRAFFIC and the problems of unhelpful parking were already becoming apparent by the 1920s. Today Magdalen Bridge carries an enormous volume of traffic in the morning and evening rush-hours. Photograph c. 1924. (OL.)

THE APPROACH FROM THE SOUTH, over Folly Bridge and along St Aldates to Carfax; Christ Church on the right. c. 1900. (OL.)

THE CITY IS SEPARATED FROM THE THAMES TO THE SOUTH by the wide spaces of Christ Church Meadow and Merton Field. Christ Church, the Cathedral and Merton College, c. 1900. (OL.)

ON THE NORTH SIDE, the roads from Woodstock and Banbury join to form broad St Giles. The view from the tower of St Mary Magdalen, c. 1890. (BL.)

THE APPROACH FROM THE WEST has long been the least imposing way into the city. The Western Region station, built in 1850 and familiar to generations of undergraduates was replaced in the early 1970s. Photograph August 1945. (BL.)

THE CENTRE OF OXFORD'S SKYLINE, close-up: looking from Queen's College to St Mary's spire, the Radcliffe Camera and Hawksmoor's towers at All Souls, c. 1880. (BL.)

SECTION TWO

The University in the City

THE CLASSIC VIEW ALONG HIGH STREET from the top of Magdalen Tower was the first picture in many of the undergraduate photograph albums produced before the First World War. c. 1905. (OM.)

ST ALDATES, with Tom Tower shrouded in scaffolding, 1909. (OL.)

MAGDALEN COLLEGE AND TOWER, closing the view down High Street from the east. The lime trees, which provided a foil to the building, are now sadly gone. 1890s. (OL.)

THE HIGH, C. 1910. Queen's College, St Mary's and All Saints take the eye round the curve, with University College on the left. (OL.)

CATTE STREET, a water-cart and the old front of Hertford College, c. 1880. The central portion was filled in, with Palladian grandeur, by Thomas Jackson in the late 1880s. (OL.)

BROAD STREET, WEST END, 1875. Market carts rest on what is now a city centre car-park. (OL.)

BROAD STREET, EAST END, C. 1880. The houses on the right were demolished soon afterwards to make way for a building which was in turn replaced, in the early 1960s, by the present bookshop and college rooms. (OL.)

TURL STREET, looking south past Lincoln College to All Saints Church, c. 1885. (OL.)

WHERE THE NEW BODLEIAN LIBRARY STANDS. These sixteenth- and seventeenth-century houses at the east end of Broad Street were just some of the many which have been sacrificed over the centuries to make way for the growing University and its colleges. Photographed 1936. (OL.)

THE CORNER OF CATTE STREET AND NEW COLLEGE LANE, c. 1880. All this has gone for Hertford College and the Indian Institute, apart from the small white building behind the lamp-post. This is the early sixteenth-century Chapel of our Lady (see p. 23). (OL.)

SEAL'S COFFEE HOUSE on the corner of Catte Street and Holywell, c. 1883. In Vanbrugh-esque style, if not by Vanbrugh, it was demolished soon after to make way for the Indian Institute; the posters advertise the sale of materials from the demolition. (OL.)

A SECTION OF THE MEDIEVAL TOWN WALL was revealed in 1899 in front of the Bodleian Library. The line of the walls is now laid out on the ground. (OL.)

THE CHAPEL OF OUR LADY, uncovered during demolition of houses for Hertford College in 1902. The chapel was 'restored' and incorporated in the new buildings. (OL.)

PARKS ROAD, c. 1865. The fence on the right is the site of the house of the Warden of Keble College. In the distance can be seen the posts which prevented wheeled traffic from coming along the road. Anyone driving to the museum had to apply at Wadham for a key to unlock one of the posts. (BL.)

THE OPEN COUNTRY north of St Giles was already being filled up with streets of Victorian Gothic houses by the 1850s. The houses were occupied mostly by wealthy townspeople and a few University professors until, in 1877, college fellows were allowed to marry and a new demand for large family houses was created. Five Bradmore Road on the Norham Manor Estate, c. 1900. (OL.)

NORTH OXFORD'S OWN PARISH CHURCH, SS. Philip and James, from Leckford Road, 1911. Designed by G.E. Street and built in the early 1860s.

SECTION THREE

The Colleges

ALL SOULS: the chapel reredos during restoration, 1872. The restoration, by Scott, retained some of the fifteenth-century framework, with new figures. (OL.)

ALL SOULS: the north quad, dominated by the Radcliffe Camera, c. 1865. (OL.)

BALLIOL COLLEGE: the old gate tower, late fifteenth century, before rebuilding, c. 1860. (OL.)

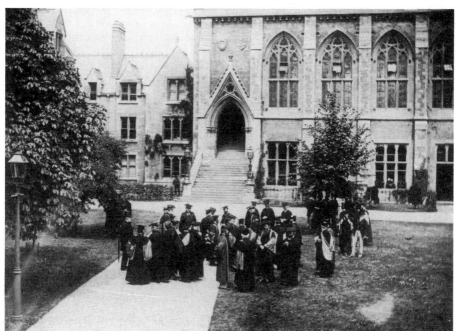

BALLIOL: the new hall of 1876–7, with a gathering of dons. Photograph by Taunt, 30 June 1886. (OL.)

BALLIOL: THE OLD FRONT, c. 1865. The section on the right was built c. 1790, but was already decaying badly. (OL.)

BALLIOL'S NEW BUILDINGS as eventually completed by Waterhouse in the 1860s and photographed in the 1880s. (OL.)

BRASENOSE COLLEGE: the front on to Radcliffe Square with the Radcliffe Camera behind its railings to the right. (OL.)

BRASENOSE: view from the area of the New Quad, past the chapel to the Radcliffe Camera, c. 1880. The buildings on the left have gone. (OL.)

CHRIST CHURCH: Dr Fell's Tower, photographed c. 1870, before the additions made to it in the late 1870s. (OL.)

CHRIST CHURCH'S BACK DOOR, Canterbury Gate, photographed by Taunt from Oriel Square c. 1880. (OL.)

THE BELFRY TOWER being built at Christ Church in the late 1870s. It was hoped the substantial structure would be both meet – appropriate – and safe and it became known as the Meat Safe. Photographs by Taunt, 1879–80. (OL.)

CORPUS CHRISTI COLLEGE, the Front Quad, c. 1885. The sundial, surmounted by the pelican, was added in 1585. (OL.)

EXETER COLLEGE CHAPEL was replaced in 1866–9: here the lower stages are seen under construction. (BL.)

EXETER OLD CHAPEL, photographed c. 1865. (OL.)

EXETER'S NEW CHAPEL, based on the Ste. Chapelle in Paris and considered by some an 'ungenial exotic' unsuited to Oxford. Photographed when new, 1869. (OL.)

HERTFORD COLLEGE'S MAIN GATE from Catte Street, demolished in 1886 to make way for Jackson's new front. Photograph c. 1880. (OL.)

KEBLE COLLEGE, Oxford's first new college for over a century – and startlingly new, all brick in a stone-built University. Designed by Butterfield, built 1868–82: the main front, c. 1890. (OL.)

KEBLE CHAPEL FROM THE UNIVERSITY PARKS, c. 1885. In a decorative college, the chapel is even more richly patterned. (OL.)

WHILE THE CHAPEL WAS BEING BUILT, a temporary one was needed at Keble, very utilitarian and in stark contrast to what replaced it. 1870s. (OL.)

KEBLE CHAPEL COMPLETED. Photograph c. 1880, looking east. (OL.)

OLD BUILDINGS facing the garden at Lincoln College, c. 1875. (OL.)

PUGIN'S GATEWAY TO MAGDALEN COLLEGE from the Gravel Walk, photographed c. 1865. Built in 1844/5 to replace an earlier one, it was in turn replaced, by the present entrance, directly off High Street in 1885. (OL.)

THE OLD PRESIDENT'S LODGINGS AT MAGDALEN, c. 1885. Very shortly afterwards they were replaced by the present lodgings, designed by Bodley and Garner. (OL.)

THE CLOISTERS OF MAGDALEN UNDER SNOW, 1866. The buttresses carry heraldic figures and fantastic beasts, put up in 1508/9 and painted, at least twice, during the seventeenth century. (OL.)

THE VIEW FROM MAGDALEN TOWER, north over the cloisters, New Buildings, Magdalen Grove and the Cherwell Valley. Photographed by Taunt c. 1875, the view today is virtually unchanged. (OL.)

MERTON COLLEGE FROM MERTON FIELD, 30 April 1908. It snowed heavily on 24 and 25 April, with subsequent flooding. Merton is separated from the open spaces by the old town wall and by Deadman's Walk, which runs along the front. (OL.)

NEW COLLEGE, GARDEN QUAD. C. 1885. The buildings of the quad are seen from the garden through the screen and gates of 1711. (OL.)

NEW COLLEGE CHAPEL, BELL TOWER AND THE OLD TOWN WALL. When the college developed outside the wall in the 1870s, these Old Slype cottages and workshops were demolished, along with a whole range on Holywell Street, for the new Holywell Buildings. Photograph c. 1870. (OL.)

ORIEL COLLEGE, THE FRONT QUAD, c. 1870. By this date the seventeenth-century Oxford Gothic buildings, of the poor Headington stone, were already wonderfully decayed. (OL.)

THE HIGH STREET FRONT OF THE QUEEN'S COLLEGE, 1870s, one of Oxford's most impressive façades, here much less disfigured by the waiting cabmen than by today's buses and bus stops. (OL.)

ST JOHN'S COLLEGE: old houses on the site of the Dolphin Inn, St Giles, bought by the college in the 1850s and 60s and used as undergraduate rooms until demolished in the late 1870s, c. 1875. (OL.)

ST JOHN'S, the gate from the gardens through to Canterbury Quad, photographed by Taunt c. 1870. (OL.)

THE BROAD STREET FRONT OF TRINITY COLLEGE, c. 1880. The seventeenth-century houses at Trinity, in a prime site for development as a grand college range, miraculously survive. (OL.)

THE GARDEN QUAD OF TRINITY, 1850s. The quad looks down the long vista of lawns and shrubs to the great iron gates on Parks Road. (BL.)

THE GATE TOWER AND CHAPEL OF TRINITY, built in the early 1690s and photographed c. 1875. The wall on the right, relic of a seventeenth-century arrangement, was swept away for the new quad buildings of the 1880s. (OL.)

THE LODGE COTTAGE OF TRINITY, photographed in the 1890s. (OL.)

VIEW THROUGH THE MAIN FRONT GATE OF UNIVERSITY COLLEGE to the south range, c. 1890. (OL.)

WORCESTER COLLEGE, the eighteenth-century entrance block, with shrubs and creeper in the forecourt, c. 1875. (OL.)

SURVIVING RANGE OF GLOUCESTER COLLEGE, Worcester's predecessor on the site. These fifteenth-century buildings comprised separate units, each the responsibility of a different distant monastery. (OL.)

ST HILDA'S COLLEGE, founded in 1893 in existing buildings, was one of four halls for women students established in Oxford in the late nineteenth century. This view, from Magdalen Bridge, c. 1895, shows the college's fine setting above the Cherwell. (OL.)

NUFFIELD COLLEGE, less than half-built when photographed in August 1950. Lord Nuffield endowed a college for graduates in 1937, but the interruption of war delayed building for more than a decade. (OL.)

University Institutions

THE GREAT GATE TOWER TO THE SCHOOLS QUADRANGLE, now part of the Bodleian Library, photographed c. 1880, before restoration. (OL.)

THE WEST RANGE OF THE SCHOOLS QUADRANGLE, built by Thomas Bodley in 1610–12 as an entrance to his library and to the existing Divinity School. Photograph c. 1876. (OL.)

THE DIVINITY SCHOOL, photographed in 1890. Above the Divinity School is Duke Humphrey's Library, which Bodley restored and re-stocked with books. (OL.)

THE BODLEIAN LIBRARY AND RADCLIFFE CAMERA, photographed from an upper window of Hertford College c. 1880, before re-modelling of the college's front range. (OL.)

ARTS END OF THE BODLEIAN LIBRARY, 1913. The thickly clustered portraits are no longer there, but little else has changed. (OL.)

ARTS END, THE DIVINITY SCHOOL AND DUKE HUMPHREY'S LIBRARY from Exeter College Garden, heavily hung with creeper in the 1870s. (OL.)

PRINTERS AT WORK in one of the tower rooms of the Bodleian Library in 1910. (OL.)

THE CORNER OF BROAD STREET AND PARKS ROAD: the hole excavated after demolition of the old houses, into which the New Bodleian Library would be placed. February 1937. (BL.)

ERECTION OF THE STEEL FRAMEWORK FOR THE NEW BODLEIAN, June 1938. (BL.)

OPENING OF THE NEW BODLEIAN by George VI, 24 October 1946. The silver key broke in the lock, but eventually the door was opened. (OL.)

THE NEW BODLEIAN looking uncharacteristically romantic in the morning sunlight. September 1954. (OL.)

THE EMPERORS, Clarendon Building and a half-completed Indian Institute, c. 1890. (OL.)

THE CLARENDON BUILDING AND SHELDONIAN THEATRE from the end of New College Lane, c. 1895. (OL.)

THE OLD CONGREGATION HOUSE OF THE UNIVERSITY, attached to St Mary's Church in the 1320s to accommodate University meetings. It is here being used to store the statues taken down from the spire in Sir Thomas Jackson's restoration of the 1890s. The statues are now in the cloisters of New College. Photograph c. 1898.

ST MARY-THE-VIRGIN, the University Church, c. 1880. On the left are shops demolished to make way for Brasenose College's new quadrangle not long afterwards. (OL.)

THE INTERIOR OF THE CATHEDRAL, looking east towards the choir. The photograph, taken c. 1870, shows the large east window of 1853, replaced in Scott's restoration of the 1870s. (OL.)

ON THE LEFT, part of Jackson's Examination Schools; on the right, Frank Cooper's Marmalade Shop. c. 1900. (OL.)

INTERIOR OF THE EXAMINATION SCHOOLS, set out for an examination, c. 1885. (OL.)

THE RADCLIFFE OBSERVATORY, late eighteenth century. The tower (above, OL) and the old observatory house (below, OM) with the astronomer's lodgings beyond. Both photographs c. 1860. (OL.)

THE UNIVERSITY PRESS IN WALTON STREET, photographed c. 1880. The Press moved here from the Clarendon Building in 1831. (OL.)

THE UNIVERSITY PRESS BINDERY, c. 1930. (OL.)

CEREMONIAL STONE-LAYING on the Indian Institute Building, 1883. (OL.)

SECTION FIVE

Vistas and Gardens

MAGDALEN TOWER across an arm of the Cherwell near to Milham Ford, with the Botanical Gardens in the middle distance. Taunt photograph, c. 1870. (OL.)

MEADOW BUILDINGS, Christ Church, from the New Walk, under snow c. 1870. (OL.)

THE WATER WALKS, Magdalen c. 1885. (OL.)

THE GREAT WYCH ELM in Magdalen Grove, 1900. (OL.)

NICHOLAS STONES' DANBY GATE to the Botanical Gardens, 1632, photographed c. 1870. (OL.)

THE FOUNTAIN in the Botanical Gardens, looking north to the Danby Gate, c. 1875. (OL.)

THE WATER-LILY HOUSE, Botanical Gardens, c. 1870. (OL.)

THE BOTANICAL GARDENS from the Cherwell, 1910. (OL.)

WORCESTER COLLEGE GARDENS, by the lake c. 1885. Worcester has Oxford's only garden truly landscaped in the informal eighteenth-century style. (OL.)

STRANGELY FURTIVE AMIDST THE CREEPER, one of the sculpted groups in Magdalen cloister, c. 1880. (OL.)

IRON GATE PIER, Magdalen College exit to the water walks, September 1901. (OL.)

College and University Life

THE UNDERGRADUATE: H.G. Hopkins was at Corpus Christi College from 1858 to 1862, and was in the University VIII in his last year. He died, aged 81, in 1920. (BL.)

THE NEW INTAKE: University College freshmen, 1904. This is a very small group compared with today's annual influx to the colleges. (OL.)

THE UNDERGRADUATE COMMUNITY: University College Common Room – all the undergraduate members – in 1906. (OL.)

ROOMS IN COLLEGE. Most sets comprised a sitting room/study and a bedroom, though standards varied very much from college to college. This room is at Lincoln College, c. 1900. (OL.)

STUDENT'S ROOM AT SOMERVILLE, founded for women in 1869. Taunt photograph, c. 1895. (OL.)

RUSKIN COLLEGE, for worker students, never became a formal part of the University. Student's study/bedroom, June 1937. (OL.)

MERTON, the finest of the early college libraries. Photograph by Henry Taunt, c. 1890. (OL.)

EARLY SIXTEENTH-CENTURY BOOKSHELVES at Merton, with a rare survival of an original arrangement: chained books to prevent loss of an expensive resource. May 1913. (OL.)

THE CENTRE OF COLLEGE LIFE, where all members of the college came together at least once a day. Hertford College Hall, photographed c. 1890, set out for a special occasion. Normal conditions were, and are, much simpler. (OL.)

NEW COLLEGE KITCHENS, June 1901. Spit-roasting at the great fires, long carried on in colleges as it had been done in the great domestic households of the Middle Ages. (OL.)

ORIEL HALL, C. 1875: high table for the fellows on a raised dais, the long tables for junior members of college. (OL.)

DONS: Balliol College, 1895. The Master, E. Caird, elected 1893, is second from the left. (OL.)

THE CHAPEL OF PEMBROKE COLLEGE, 1899. Chapel was a compulsory part of college life in some colleges until after the Second World War. (OL.)

CHRIST CHURCH CATHEDRAL CHORISTERS in Tom Quad, April 1941. (OL.)

THE COLLEGE SERVANTS, St John's, 1895. (James Bond.)

DONS: Herbert Wilson Greene, Fellow and Tutor of Magdalen, 1888–1910, and twice Vice-President, in his rooms in New Buildings, 12 May 1903. (BL.)

RUSKIN STUDENTS were outside the tight class structures of the old colleges; washing-up, 1906. (OL.)

PASSAGE AT THE HEAD OF THE STAIRS, Brasenose College, 1889. Associated with Verdant Greene, Cuthbert Bede's fictional hero, who gives a splendid evocation of Oxford undergraduate life in the 1850s. (OL.)

THE OUTDOOR PULPIT at Magdalen College. The custom of an annual sermon on the feast of St John the Baptist, long discontinued, was revived in 1896. 14 June 1922. (OL.)

THE PRESIDENT OF MAGDALEN'S GARDEN, looking east to the Tower, c. 1875. (OL.)

THE SENIOR COMMON ROOM of Corpus Christi College, 1908. (OL.)

THE PRINCIPAL OF SOMERVILLE, Miss A.C. Maitland, in her rooms in college, 1895. (OL.)

THE END OF THE SECOND WORLD WAR brought an older and more experienced than average group of undergraduates to the University. Morning coffee at Merton, 1947. (OL.)

THE UNIVERSAL MEANS OF TRANSPORT: bicycles in the High Street arcade of Queen's College, 1903. (OL.)

ARRIVING FOR A UNIVERSITY LECTURE, Examination Schools, 1950. In the reliefs to left and right of the arch: the viva voce examination and the conferral of a degree. (OL.)

UNDERGRADUATES IN THE HIGH, 1930s. (OL.)

IN THE GARDEN, University College, c. 1905. (OL.)

SOME UNDERGRADUATES spent a year living outside college. 'The Digs, 7 King Edward Street, Summer 1909'; a group from University College. (OL.)

TAKING WORK (TOP) AND TEA into the garden at Somerville, 1895. (OL.)

IN THE 1870s and 80s the University began tentatively to offer opportunities for study to those 'outside'. One method was the Summer School at Oxford; here a group of external students is photographed on the steps of Balliol Hall in 1887. From such beginnings grew the present External Studies Department of the University. (OL.)

ONE OF THE NUMEROUS COLLEGE AND UNIVERSITY SOCIETIES which came and went, or continued to flourish: the Shakespeare Club at University College, 1909. (OL.)

THE OXFORD UNION was a place to escape from the confines of college life, to read, discuss and debate. The buildings of the Union, c. 1885. (OL.)

EX-PRESIDENT NIXON visits to speak at the Oxford Union, 1 December 1978 (*Oxford Mail and Times*).

Ceremonies and Celebrations

THE ENCAENIA is the University's great annual celebration, at the end of Summer (Trinity) Term. Here the procession to Encaenia was photographed by Henry Taunt as it passed Queen's College in 1897. (OL.)

ENCAENIA PROCESSION outside All Souls, with Chancellor Curzon preceded by the University officials. *c.* 1908. (OL.)

DEGREE CEREMONY IN THE SHELDONIAN THEATRE, 14 October 1920. Women had been allowed to study for and to take examinations since 1894, but not, until 1920, to take degrees. On this occasion over fifty took their degrees, 'among them being staff of various colleges'. (BL.)

THE MAY MORNING HYMN from the top of Magdalen Tower, 1895. (OL.)

THE CROWDS BELOW ON MAGDALEN BRIDGE. Both photographs by Henry Taunt. (OL.)

THE COMMEMORATION BALL, traditionally held at each college once every three years at the end of the summer term. They usually ended with the formal group photograph: early morning after the Magdalen Commem., June 1908. (OL.)

THE MORNING AFTER (7.00 a.m.) the University College Commemoration Ball, 1909. (OL.)

FAMILIES OF UNDERGRADUATES came up to Oxford for the Commemoration celebrations. With a shortage of suitable partners in Oxford, friends' sisters were particularly welcome. Group at University College, 1909. (OL.)

PREPARATION OF THE BOAR'S HEAD for the traditional Christmas ceremony at the Queen's College, c. 1900. It is said to celebrate the deliverance of an early clerk of the college from an angry wild boar. He escaped by forcing his copy of Aristotle down the animal's throat. (OL.)

PROCLAMATION to the University of the accession of Edward VII, outside St Mary's, 1901. There was a separate proclamation to the town. (OL.)

Leisure, Sports and Games

PICNIC AT NUNEHAM COURTENAY, after rowing down the river from Oxford, 28 June 1890.
H.W. Greene is kneeling, left, with sisters and friends. (BL.)

ARCHERY PRACTICE in the gardens of St John's College, 1863. (OL.)

THE TROUT INN AT GODSTOW, target for many water- and land-based undergraduate expeditions, c. 1890. (OL.)

CROQUET PARTY IN THE GARDEN. The Spiers family and guests in their garden off St Giles, 4 September 1856. (BL.)

PICNIC ON THE BANKS OF THE CHERWELL, 26 June 1905. H.W. Greene and party, from Magdalen during the college's Commem. that year. (BL.)

DRESSING UP: children's Christmas party, provided in December 1905 by undergraduates at University College. (OL.)

THE CAST of the Oxford University Dramatic Society's 1907 production, *The Taming of the Shrew*. (BL.)

UNIVERSITY COLLEGE TORPIDS RUGBY XV played Magdalen College Torpids in 1906, and drew six all. Both teams photographed together. (OL.)

EXETER COLLEGE BEAGLES out near Woodstock, 1905. A number of colleges kept packs early this century, but all have now gone. (BL.)

THE UNIVERSITY RUGBY XV, 1885–6. The annual encounter with Cambridge was, and remains, the high point of the season. (OM.)

MEMBERS OF THE ALPINE CLUB, on the roofs of University College, 1906. The faces of the members have been replaced by those of more prominent personalities: (left to right), 'William of the Clarendon', Sir William Anson, Maurice Woods, the Bishop of London and the Revd Dr Spooner. (BL.)

VINCENT'S CLUB DINNER, C. 1900. Vincent's, founded in 1863, became the leading club for sportsmen in the University, to which those who gained success in the sporting field were elected. (OL.)

OXFORD'S GREAT SPORTING MOMENT COMMEMORATED. On 6 May 1954, Roger Bannister of Exeter College ran the first ever mile under four minutes, at the Iffley Road Sports Ground. The photograph of the unveiling of a plaque, 12 May 1955, shows (left to right) Christopher Chataway, Bannister and Chris Brasher. (OL.)

THE 'BEES' CRICKET TEAM sets off from University College for a match at Wallingford, Summer 1908. (OL.)

THE 'BEES' AT WALLINGFORD. Informal cricket, against local village sides, was more relaxed than the inter-college matches. (BL.)

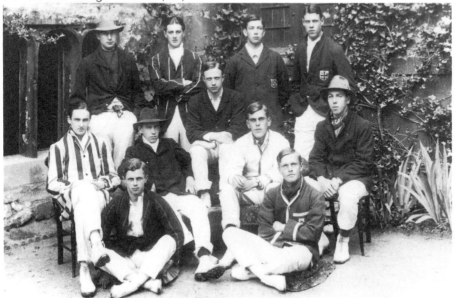

THE ST EDMUND HALL CRICKET XI, 1911. (CC.)

The River

ROWING WAS THE SUPREME OXFORD PLEASURE, with two annual competitions when crews attempted to climb the ladder by bumping the boat ahead – Torpids in February or March and Eights Week in May. The town took as much pleasure as the University in these events, and the river and towpaths were crowded. The photograph shows Eights Week, 1911. (OM.)

THE RACES START ABOVE IFFLEY LOCK, the boats setting out in the order in which they finished the last time. Lincoln, Pembroke and Exeter boats, Eights Week, 1907. (OL.)

THE STARTING GUNS, with Mr Thomas Timms, the University Waterman, 1890s. (OL.)

EIGHTS WEEK, c. 1905. A bump has taken place near the mouth of the New Cut. (OL.)

THOMAS TIMMS, University Waterman, 1890s. (OL.)

A CREW ON THE TOWPATH, 1930s. (OL.)

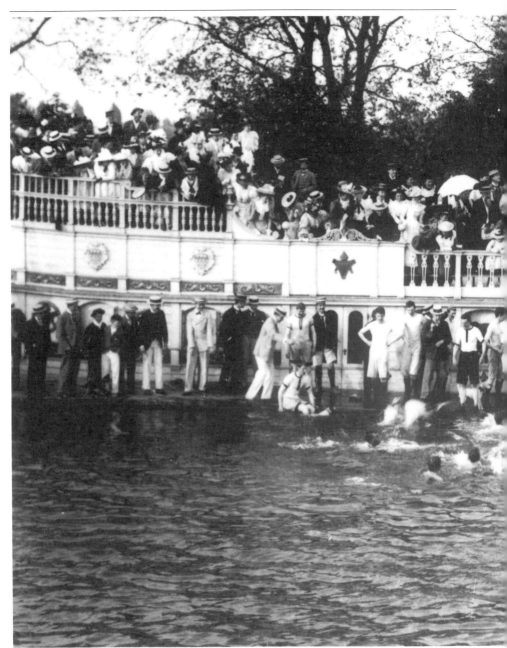

THE COLLEGE BARGES, moored along the towpath by Christ Church Meadow, served as clubhouses for the oarsmen and grandstands for privileged spectators: Magdalen College barge, Wednesday, 29 May 1895. It was a damp day, not just for those in the river; rain fell all through Eights Week that year. (BL.)

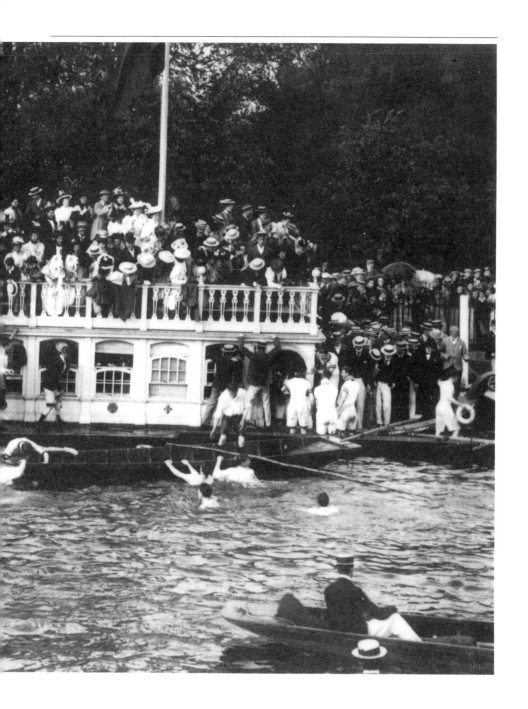

RELAXATION INSIDE THE QUEEN'S COLLEGE BARGE, 1898. (OL.)

EIGHTS WEEK, 1910. Note the photographer, precarious on his step-ladder, on the right. (OL.)

TORPIDS COULD NOT TAKE PLACE in 1895, as the river was frozen. Corpus Christi improvised a boat on the ice. (OL.)

THE UNIVERSITY BOAT RACE VIII, 3 April 1909. Oxford beat Cambridge by 3½ lengths. (OL.)

THE UNIVERSITY WOMEN'S BOAT CLUB VIII, March 1945. (OL.)

THE HENLEY REGATTA, after the end of Summer Term, attracted crews from Oxford, Cambridge and London, together with their supporters. On the river at Henley, 1908. (OL.)

THE UNIVERSITY BOATHOUSE, built 1880–1, photographed by Taunt c. 1890. (OL.)

THE START OF THE BOAT RACE, 1890. Oxford won. (OL.)

MORE RELAXED RIVER PLEASURES: punting – and canoeing – on the Cherwell, 1920s. (OL.)

PUNTING ALONG THE BACKWATERS OF THE CHERWELL at Lady Margaret Hall, c. 1895. (OL.)

THE VICTORIA ARMS, on the Cherwell at Marston, was a not too strenuous destination from Oxford. c. 1885. (OL.)

University People

CHRIST CHURCH UNDERGRADUATES – 'Twiss, Lane and Williams' – photographed by Charles Lutwidge Dodgson (Lewis Carroll) c. 1858–9. Dodgson, Tutor in Mathematics at Christ Church, was, among other things, an important early portrait photographer, recording many of the Oxford personalities of his time. (CC.)

DODGSON, photographed by himself, or by a friend, c. 1858–9. (CC.)

SARAH ACLAND, daughter of Sir Henry Acland, was an important amateur photographer who recorded many of her father's friends in the 1890s. Two here are the Marquis of Salisbury (Chancellor, 1869–1903) taken in 1894, and W.E. Gladstone, taken in 1892, early in her experience of photography. She recorded, 'Had I at the time photographed for three years I should have been afraid to attempt it. Mr Gladstone was a most kind and patient sitter.' (BL.)

SIR HENRY ACLAND, Regius Professor of Medicine, and Henry Liddell, Dean of Christ Church (and father of Alice). Two of the leading figures in late nineteenth-century Oxford, photographed by Sarah Acland at home at 40 Broad Street, one of the houses removed for the New Bodleian. (BL.)

ACLAND'S STUDY AT BROAD STREET in the 1890s. Millais' portrait of John Ruskin hangs above the desk. Acland and Ruskin were close friends, who together worked for and planned the new University Museum in the 1850s. (BL.)

ACLAND, JOWETT AND DR WOODS OF TRINITY, outside Balliol College, c. 1890. Benjamin Jowett was a powerful figure in the University who, as Master of Balliol, set out to make his college the most intellectually successful and influential. He disliked being photographed, and the expressions of all three suggest they were caught unawares by Henry Taunt, slipping out from his shop across the road. (BL.)

THE COLLEGE PORTER EXERTED HIS OWN FORM OF POWER. John Bossom was for many years Porter of Brasenose, photographed 14 April 1860. (BL.)

BULLDOGS, the University's police, who assist the Proctors in keeping order in what, periodically, can be a turbulent institution. May 1983. (*Oxford Mail and Times.*)

THE PRESIDENT AND FELLOWS OF MAGDALEN COLLEGE, photographed before installation of the President T.H. Warren, as Vice-Chancellor, 9 October 1906. (BL.)

EDWARD VII, as Prince of Wales, was an undergraduate at Christ Church from October 1859 until December 1860. He lived, not in college, but at Frewin Hall, New Inn Hall Street, where the photograph was taken. Here (standing) he is seen with General Bruce, Herbert Fisher and Lt. Col. Keppel. (BL.)

HIS GRANDSON, Edward Prince of Wales, was at Magdalen for rather longer and lived in college, from 1912 until the outbreak of war in 1914. Photograph 1912. (OL.)

OXFORD STONEMASONS, at the top of Tom Tower, Christ Church, on completion of restoration, 1909. (OL.)

BISHOP SAMUEL WILBERFORCE, Oxford's fundamentalist bishop, who clashed with Thomas Huxley at the University Museum on the subject of evolution in 1860. Photograph taken about that time. (BL.)

SERVANTS OF THE UNIVERSITY MUSEUM, 1882. (OL.)

EXETER COLLEGE PERSONALITIES. The Rector, Revd Dr Lightfoot, appearing as a gorilla, accompanied by the Sub-Rector, the Revd W. Ince. c. 1890. (BL.)

JOHN RUSKIN'S SCHEME for the improvement of the road at North Hinksey was introduced to encourage undergraduates in useful community works and the virtues of honest toil; photograph 1874 (BL). Oscar Wilde, at Magdalen College, was one of those who laboured for a short time, but the long-term value of the project was limited. (BL.)

The Museums

THE EARLIEST UNIVERSITY GALLERIES were around the Schools Quadrangle. The photograph, c. 1885, shows paintings, sculpture, models and, below the tower, the statue of the Earl of Pembroke, now outside in the Quadrangle. (OL.)

OXFORD'S (AND BRITAIN'S) EARLIEST PUBLIC MUSEUM, the Ashmolean, opened in 1683. Photograph c. 1890. Now the Old Ashmolean, housing the Museum of the History of Science. (OL.)

THE OLD ASHMOLEAN'S FRONTAGE facing the Sheldonian, c. 1855. The wall on the left had niches to house the Arundel Marbles from the University's sculpture collection. (BL.)

DISPLAYS OF ANTIQUITIES in the colonnaded main entrance gallery of the Old Ashmolean, 1870s. Elias Ashmole's portrait hangs over the fireplace.

THE TAYLOR INSTITUTE and, beyond, the University Galleries, built in the 1840s, photographed in the 1890s. As material was transferred it became, by 1908, the new Ashmolean. (OL.)

STAIRCASE in the (new) Ashmolean, 1899, with Ashmole's portrait in its new position over the stairwell. (OL.)

A NEW MUSEUM, for the study of science, was promoted by Acland and Ruskin and built in 1855–60, in isolation from the old University. The University Museum completed (above, 1860, OL) and under construction (below). (UM.)

MAN'S RELATIONSHIP TO THE APES, display case in the University Museum, 1890s. (UM.)

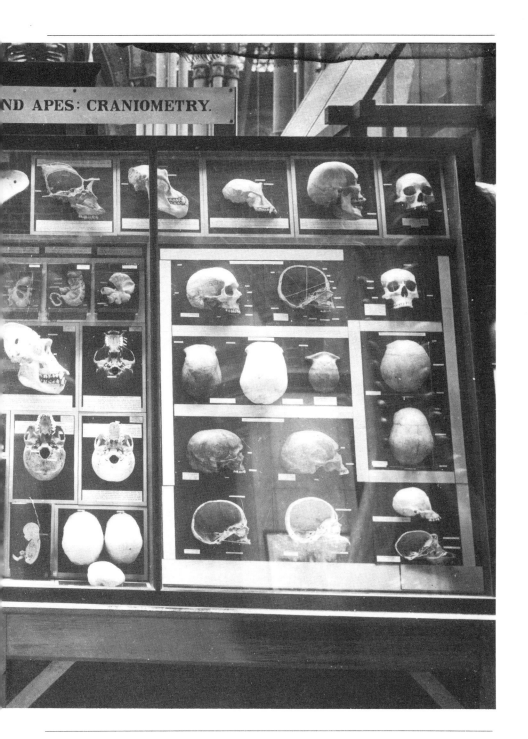

INTERIOR OF THE UNIVERSITY MUSEUM, late nineteenth century: bare brickwork, naturalistic ironwork and a vast glass roof. (OL.)

IN 1885–6, another new museum was built, on the back of the University Museum, to house General Pitt Rivers' gift of his collection of ethnographical material. The museum displays, photographed in 1915. (OL.)

MUSEUM LODGE, on the corner of Parks Road and South Parks Road, 1901. The lodge was demolished, to make way for the Radcliffe Science Library, in the 1930s. (OL.)

HENRY BALFOUR, Curator of the Pitt Rivers Museum, with three students for the Diploma in Anthropology, in the Upper Gallery of the museum, 1908. Balfour was Curator for 48 years, from 1891 until his death in 1939. (Pitt Rivers Museum.)

Training for War

OXFORD UNIVERSITY VOLUNTEER CORPS, parading in 1897. (OL.)

THE COMMUNICATION COMPANY OF OUOTC, on parade near Aldershot, 1912. (OM.)

OUOTC CAMP AT ALDERSHOT, 1912. The destruction of a tent by fire is causing some bemusement. Soon a whole generation of undergraduates would disappear into the First World War. For five years the University must have felt very empty. (OM.)

THE WARRIORS RETURN. Chancellor Curzon at the Encaenia of 1919 with (front row, left to right) Wemyss, Honnash, Pershing, Joffre, Haig, Beatty, Hoover, Wilson, coming to Oxford to receive their honorary degrees. (OL.)

SPIKES. SNAPDRAGONS AND OLD STONEWORK; a wall of Trinity College, July 1912. (OL.)

ACKNOWLEDGEMENTS

For permission to reproduce material in their possession, grateful acknowledgement is made to:

Bodleian Library, Oxford ● Mr James Bond ● the Governing Body of Christ Church, Oxford ● *Oxford Mail and Times* ● Oxfordshire Museums, Woodstock ● Pitt Rivers Museum, Oxford ● University Museum, Oxford.

The source of each photograph has been identified within the caption, using the following key:

BL   : Bodleian Library, Oxford
CC   : the Governing Body of Christ Church, Oxford
OM   : Oxfordshire Museums, Woodstock
OL   : Oxfordshire Libraries, Central Library, Westgate, Oxford
UM   : University Museum, Oxford